Trailblazers!

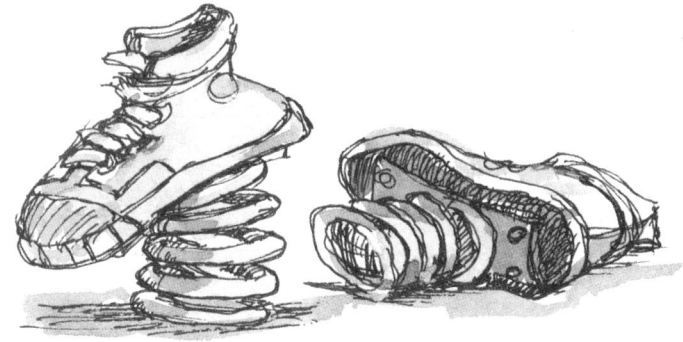

Contents

Chapter 1	5
Chapter 2	13
Chapter 3	21
Chapter 4	30
Chapter 5	37
Chapter 6	46
Chapter 7	54
Chapter 8	65
Chapter 9	77
Chapter 10	85

Chapter 1

It's Miss Soames's crazy plan that starts it all. Starts turning my best friend into my worst enemy. That and the new girl, Duana O'Neill.

Joel and I are walking home from school, talking about Miss Soames's latest idea. She wants us to help some kids whose families lost their homes because of a flash flood. She's got this brilliant plan about the school doing this sponsored walk-a-thon and raising lots of money.

"But I hate walking," moans Joel.

"Don't you want to help save those kids?" I ask.

"Yeah. But I'm not doing anything to save Tracy Duke. She's too weird."

He's right. Tracy Duke is a bit strange. I don't know why, but she's always staring at something as though it's going to disappear for some reason. And that's not all. She's always the first one to put her hand up whenever Miss Soames wants something done.

"We're not going to be saving us," I explain. "It's for the kids who had that flood they've been talking about on the news." I kick at a stone on the footpath. "Besides, we don't want Room Three to win."

Joel makes a sad face. "They're going to win anyway."

He's right, I know that. The whole world knows that Room Three always wins everything. Room Three always makes the most money when we do this kind of stuff. But, still, you've got to hope. There's bound to be a first time they don't win something.

Joel interrupts my thoughts.

"Do you know how many kids were in that flood?" Joel asks.

"No."

"Then how are we going to know how far we've got to walk, if we don't know how many kids we need to save?"

Joel's always thinking of things like that. He's really smart, especially at maths and computers. He's going to be an inventor when he grows up. Last month, he made an aluminium can smasher. When he tried it out on a pile of empty cans, it landed on his foot.

His foot had to be X-rayed. Nothing was broken, but he got a huge purple bruise. Even though Joel's my best friend, I have to say that he's totally hopeless at anything that has to do with sports.

My best subject is table tennis. But Miss Soames told me table tennis doesn't count as a school subject. Miss Soames said it has to be something like reading or writing. But I'm not very good at those. After table tennis, the next best thing I do is imitating animals. Once when I was pretending to be a dog, I even had Miss Soames fooled for a while. Until some of the kids in Room Three gave me away. I had to stay in at lunchtime and put away library books.

"I don't know how walking is supposed to help anyone. It'll probably kill me," grumbles Joel. "Nine and a half is too young to die!"

Joel and I are the same age. He moved here two years ago. We became friends right away. Then we discovered that we had the same birthday – the eighth of October. I thought we might be twins, and that's why we're good at different things. He's got the smart part of my brain, and I've got the sports part of his. But Mum put a stop to that idea. She told me that when I was born, there was definitely only one baby.

"A walk-a-thon sounds mega boring," complains Joel.

I think for a second and then say, "Why don't you drop your can smasher on your foot again? Then Miss Soames couldn't make you go on the walk. Not if your toes are broken."

"I can't. Dad locked it up. And he locked up his tools, too."

"How are you going to do your inventing?"

Joel shrugs. Then, after a minute, he says, "Maybe Miss Soames would let me be the counting person. She's got to have one."

"What? You mean counting the money?"

"Yeah. And the kilometres. Stuff like that."

I don't like to say it, but I don't think Joel's got much of a chance. Miss Soames likes to do everything herself. "She might," I say doubtfully.

Miss Soames is a very big person with short barbed-wire hair and little lips. If she gives you a squeeze around the shoulders when you've done something good, you can feel your bones starting to crumble. Most of the time she's OK, but when she's angry she shakes like a volcano made out of jelly.

Joel sighs long and loud. "It's stupid! We're going to have to walk the whole trail ten hundred times to beat Room Three."

"Yeah. I know."

We both walk slowly, side by side, up Dee Street. At the far end is Wangs Supermarket. Mum and Dad work there. I turn to Joel. "Do you want some bubblegum?"

Joel's face brightens. "OK."

We go into Wangs. I go straight to the confectionery and pick two packets of green

gum. It's the kind that explodes when you chew it. I go up to Dad. He's the checkout person in the express lane. The women at the supermarket tease him for being the only man on the checkout. Dad doesn't care. He says it's one of the best jobs he's ever had. Mum got it for him. She's one of Wangs's bigwigs.

"Hi, kids," says Dad, grinning.

"Hi, Dad. We've got to go walking," I tell him, putting down the gum.

"Hello, Mr Turner."

Dad digs in his pocket for some money. "Matt, this is the last gum this week."

I nod. I'm not bothered. He says the same thing every day.

"You won't want to go walking this weekend," says Dad. "Marla's coming over."

"Oh, boy. Is she? When? Tonight?"

"Hold your horses," laughs Dad.

Marla's my half-sister. She's been away for weeks, working in a forest, thinning pine trees. She doesn't live with us. She's too old for that.

"I'd rather go surfing," mutters Joel, "not walking."

Dad looks mystified. "Surfing? It's too cold for that."

"Not at the beach, Dad. He means on the computer. If he had one."

At that moment, a customer comes up behind us. She plonks her plastic basket down and starts taking out her shopping.

Dad winks then says, "What's all this about walking?"

"It's all Miss Soames's idea…" starts Joel.

I cut in. "The whole school's got to do it."

The customer clears her throat.

"Tell me about it tonight," says Dad, pulling a packet of rice towards him. "See you later."

We put some gum in our mouths and chew it hard. It starts to explode as we leave the supermarket.

Chapter 2

My sister Marla was born in the olden days when my mum was married to Jim. Marla is eighteen. Jim's not my father though. My dad is the one who works in the supermarket. I have another sister, too. Her name is Stephanie, but I call her Short-Stuff. She is nine months old.

Short-Stuff goes to work every day with Mum and Dad. She stays at the crèche in the supermarket. Talk about a noisy place. There are so many kids – more than all the peas in a big packet of frozen peas. I try not to go in there. Too many kids running around everywhere. What a disaster area! The crèche was Mum's idea. I guess it's an OK place if you can handle all that noise.

After dinner that night, I tell Mum about the walking thing.

"That sounds great," she says in her excited voice.

Mum is always enthusiastic about causes.

One time she took me marching down the main street with lots of other people. (I was little at the time, but I still remember it.) She was into saving the country schools. I don't think they saved many. Since then she's been busy saving insects and trees. Now she's into saving parents.

"The walk-a-thon is going to be on Pine Trail," I tell her, wanting sympathy. Everyone knows Pine Trail is a killer. Even Marla said so after she'd been on it. And if you knew Marla, you'd know she wasn't kidding. Marla's a sports freak. She's good at practically every sport there is. She's got muscles by the dozens and can ripple them like waves.

Mum nods her faraway nod. I know she's not really listening; instead, she's thinking about her causes. Mum's really pretty. She has lots of curls, not done by the hairdressers like other mums. Her hair is orange. Not as orange as an orange, but that sort of colour. When she moves her head, her curls bounce. I like that. It's nice. The only thing that's kind of weird is her front teeth. When she was sixteen, she fell off her boyfriend's bike. Since then she's had false teeth.

Dad comes into the kitchen with a giggling Short-Stuff balanced on his shoulders. "Tell me about the walk-a-thon, Matt."

"It's on Pine Trail. The more we walk, the more money we make."

Short-Stuff lets out a loud burp.

"What's the money for?" asks Dad.

"Miss Soames says it's to help out the people who had that flood. We're going to raise money to buy new clothes and toys for the kids. Joel says he's not doing any walking if it's to save Tracy Duke. He thinks Tracy Duke is really weird. I think she's kind of weird, too. But I told Joel that it wasn't about Tracy Duke; it's about some other kids. He says all that walking sounds incredibly boring. But I told him that…"

Mum interrupts my rambling. "Who's sponsoring the walk?" she asks, lifting her head from the pile of work she brought home.

I shrug.

"It doesn't sound very organized," says Mum, getting a glint in her eyes.

I know that glint. So does Dad.

"Linda, you've got enough on your plate," he tells her.

Short-Stuff grabs a handful of Dad's hair and gives it a hard pull.

"Ouch!" exclaims Dad, lifting her from his shoulders and putting her down on the floor. Short-Stuff chortles and scoots along on her bottom over to the rubbish bin and starts crashing the lid up and down.

I keep on talking. I'm used to Short-Stuff interrupting me all the time. "The whole school's going to do it. The class that raises the most money gets to go on a tour of the bread factory," I say. "That was Miss Soames' idea, too."

"Dough for dough," chuckles Dad at his own joke.

"It's not funny, Dad. How would you like to have to walk for a whole day?"

"I'll sponsor you. I'll double your pocket money," says Dad in a big hurry.

"You have to pay for every kilometre," I tell him. "That could cost you a lot." I'm busy thinking about the model spaceship I've been trying to get for my birthday, but now it looks like it'll be out. Any spare money will be heading in the opposite direction.

"That's OK," says Dad. "Children are a good cause." He stops talking and rushes over to Short-Stuff who is busy throwing rubbish out of the bin onto the floor.

"It might rain," I say, looking for any possibility of the walk being cancelled.

"Then you'll probably have to walk in the rain," laughs Mum.

She's right. Once Miss Soames makes up her mind about something, she never changes it. And she is very excited about the walking plan. So it probably means even if there was a tornado on the way, we'd still have to do it.

"Do you think you can walk the whole trail?" asks Dad. He throws pieces of last night's dinner back into the rubbish bin then picks up Short-Stuff.

"Not in my old falling-apart sneakers," I say, suddenly realizing there could be a new pair in it for me.

Mum ignores my hint. "So when is this walk-a-thon?" she asks.

"Next Saturday."

Then, all of a sudden, I have this amazing idea. At least, it will be an amazing idea if we get the most money and Room Three doesn't beat us.

"Mum?" I say, nicely.

"Yes, dear."

I shudder. I hate it when she calls me that. But now isn't the time to argue, not when there's a brilliant plan in the making. "Do you think Wangs would donate a computer to the school?"

Mum sucks air in through her front false teeth. "What for?"

I explain carefully. "A computer would be a much better prize for the winning class than a trip to the bread factory."

Mum leans back in her chair and looks interested. "Ahhh. You mean get Wangs to support the walk?"

I nod. "Even Joel would walk for that."

Mum's eyes sparkle. "Wangs's Walk for Kids." Already her mind is working on the idea. "I like it. Good publicity and public relations for the supermarket and the school."

"But," I add, getting in while I can, "it'd be better if it wasn't just any old computer. The Black Arrow is the best. It does everything, plays music and all." I stop for a breath. Joel has told me all about the Black Arrow. He's got an uncle who has one. Joel gets to use it when he goes and stays with him at Christmas time.

Mum looks thoughtful. "I'll see what I can do. It's a great idea, Matt."

I grin. If Mum can get Wangs to agree, then I bet Joel would walk to the moon and back to help make sure the Black Arrow computer gets into our classroom and not Room Three's.

Mum goes back to her work, and Dad picks up Short-Stuff and carries her to her bedroom. By the time I've made myself a jam sandwich and am walking down the hall, I can hear Dad singing to Short-Stuff. Dad's hopeless at singing. It sounds more like someone squealing in pain.

I go into my bedroom and shut the door. If only Miss Soames had suggested a table tennis weekend. That would have really got Room Three worried out of their skulls. But walking! Room Three will probably walk all over us.

Chapter 3

The next morning in class, there's a surprise. A new girl stands at the front of the room. Miss Soames has her arm around the new girl's shoulder. I can feel it being crushed from where I'm sitting. But the new girl doesn't seem to notice. She is smiling. And wow! Is she pretty! What was that? I don't know what made me think like that. There's no way I'm into girls – no way. Not even if they are cool-looking and have long curly brown hair and big brown eyes.

"This is Duana O'Neill," says Miss Soames, pausing for a moment but keeping her cheery face on. "She is joining us. Let's do our best to make Duana feel at home. OK? Now who would like to be her partner for the day?"

Tracy Duke puts up her hand. She's the only one, of course. She always raises her hand for everything.

"Thank you, Tracy."

Tracy gets out of her chair and rushes up to Duana. Anyone would think the new girl was a dog the way Tracy leads her to the empty desk beside her. I slink down into my chair. It's too embarrassing. Joel gives me a sad look and crosses his eyes.

"I saw that, Joel," says Miss Soames, her happy voice wavering for a moment. When Tracy and Duana are settled, Miss Soames continues. "Now how many of you told your parents about the walk-a-thon?"

Tracy's hand goes up.

"Anyone else?" asks Miss Soames.

A few more hands straggle up. Mine as well.

"Well!" exclaims Miss Soames, bringing her little lips together. "This is a combined class effort. You'll have to do better. That effort wouldn't save a grasshopper."

I'm not sure what a grasshopper has to do with helping some people who had a flood. Sometimes Miss Soames says some funny things that have nothing to do with what she's talking about.

Miss Soames looks around the room. "Who would like to tell Duana about the walk-a-thon?" And before Tracy can get her hand up, Miss Soames adds, "Someone who hasn't had their hand up this morning."

When no one volunteers, Miss Soames looks at Joel. "Joel, as we haven't heard from you for a while, you can tell Duana all about it."

"Thanks a whole lot," mumbles Joel under his breath.

I grin.

"What was that, Joel? Speak up," says Miss Soames, sounding a bit twitchy. "And it would be nice if you turned and spoke to Duana instead of mumbling to the top of your desk."

Joel explains about the walk-a-thon, then Duana smiles and says, "Thank you, Joel."

Joel smiles back then wiggles around in his chair. Hey! What's happening here? Joel's never smiled at a girl in his whole life. At least not in the time I've known him.

Miss Soames nods. "Good." She goes over to the whiteboard. "Now before we start on our sponsor cards, I want you to think about who you would like as your walking partner."

Miss Soames never said anything yesterday about us having partners. I think she makes up the rules as she goes along. Of course, Joel and I don't need to decide about who our partners will be.

"There will be a special incentive award for the twosome who walk the trail the fastest," continues Miss Soames.

That leaves out Joel and me. We'll probably be last.

Tracy's hand goes up. "What's the incentive award, Miss Soames?"

"Ahhh," says Miss Soames, lowering her voice. "That's a secret."

That means she doesn't know. Miss Soames always uses that voice when she is still deciding about something.

For the rest of the morning, we make our sponsor cards. Miss Soames writes the heading for us:

Name   Address   Amount/KM

KM Walked   Total Amount

By the time my card is finished, it looks really neat. Above the heading, I've drawn a picture of me sitting down at the top of Pine Trail, eating a pie. When Miss Soames sees it, she says it looks more like a sit-down-a-thon than a walk-a-thon, so I erase my legs and do them again, this time making them standing up. But I keep in the pie.

Some of the kids had to start all over again. They had so many drawings on them, there wasn't room for the names of the people who were going to pay us millions for walking Pine Trail.

At morning break, Joel and I are hanging around as usual. I'm just going to tell him about my idea of getting Wangs to give the winning class a computer, when Tracy Duke and the new girl come by.

Tracy is explaining absolutely everything possible about our school as though Duana is a two-year-old.

"Over there is the teachers' staff room and the first-aid room."

As they pass us, Duana turns her head and looks in our direction. She gives Joel and me a dazzling smile.

"And over there is the gymnasium," Tracy carries on.

Suddenly Duana stops and turns. Then, looking straight at Joel, she says, "How about being my walking partner, Joel?"

I'm stunned. Can you believe it? She's been at the school for two minutes and already she's talking to Joel like he's her best friend.

And do you know what Joel does? He shrugs. He actually shrugs as though he might consider it. He doesn't say, "No thanks. Matt's my partner." No, he shuffles his feet with a stupid expression on his face.

And, besides, if she was going to ask anyone, it would have been better if she'd asked me. I'm much better at sports than Joel. Actually, everyone is much better at sports than Joel.

Then, to finish it off, Joel opens his mouth and says, "Maybe."

WHAT? MAYBE? I guess he must be getting sick or something. Mum told me last week that a lot of kids are getting chickenpox. Maybe that's it.

"Gymnastics is my favourite sport," says Duana. "Do you like gymnastics, Joel?"

Joel nods. His eyes swivel away from my thunderstruck gaze.

I can't believe what I'm hearing and seeing. Joel hates gymnastics. He hates them worse than walking. I open my mouth to say something, but Tracy gets in first.

"I'm really good at cartwheels," she announces, opening her brown eyes wide and flapping her eyelashes at Duana. When Duana doesn't scream with excitement at this bit of news, Tracy changes her expression to a sad one and says in a hurt tone, "I thought we could do the walk-a-thon together."

Before Duana can reply to this sensational invitation, a group of kids from Room Three come towards us. They are all walking fast, arms swinging and legs motoring.

"Check that out," I say. "They're training for the walk-a-thon." No one in our class has even bothered to think about doing any training. And, knowing them, they never will. I'm beginning to be sorry I asked Mum about trying to get a computer. Room Three might as well have it now and save the rest of us the trouble of walking Pine Trail. Maybe it's not too late to stop Mum asking Wangs, then Room Three would get to go to the bread factory instead. That'd teach them.

When the group passes by us, Tracy takes Duana's arm. "Come on," she says, "I've still got lots of things to show you." Then they wander off.

For the rest of the break, Joel and I don't mention what has just gone on with Duana. It's too crazy to think about. Of course Joel is going to be my partner for the walk-a-thon. The two of us are a team. And, besides, if he wasn't my partner, I might get stuck with someone like Tracy. And that would be a fate a hundred times worse than Miss Soames hugging you.

Chapter 4

Over dinner that night, Mum delivers the worst possible news. Wangs is going to give our school a computer. And that's not all. They're going to make it a Black Arrow, plus Mum has talked them into throwing in an Internet connection. Can you imagine? And if all that isn't bad enough, Wangs is going to pay for the winning class to surf the Net for a whole year.

All because of my amazing idea.

Well, our class can say goodbye to even a microdot chance of getting the computer. We seem to be the most doomed class in the universe. Last term when the swimming sports were about to happen, and our class was going to win something for the first time ever, our champion swimmer came down with the flu. Guess who won? Yeah. Room Three. Of course.

"Why so gloomy?" asks Mum. "I thought you'd be pleased. After all, it was your idea."

"I am," I say, trying to sound enthusiastic. I stab at the meatball sitting in a puddle of tomato sauce.

"Mr Wang is having some posters made," continues Mum, getting all fired up. "And we're going to have a special display in the supermarket..."

"But what about Miss Soames?" I say, suddenly remembering nothing has been said to her about the sudden change in the prize plans. "She still thinks the bread factory is it."

"Ah. Yes," says Mum, nibbling at a strand of spaghetti and frowning.

Short-Stuff squeals as she drops a lump of her meatball over the edge of the high chair and onto the floor. I feel like doing the same with mine.

"You could call her tonight and tell her," says Mum, pushing her half-full plate away.

Mum never eats the meals she's made. And I don't blame her. They're not very good. She's not that great a cook. Dad is much better, but tonight he's on late shift at the supermarket.

I stare glumly at the four remaining meatballs on my plate. They taste more like mudballs. "I've got lots of homework," I say, making it sound as though I could be up until midnight. I don't want to call Miss Soames. She might get mad at me for butting in when she's probably spent hours arranging the trip to the bakery.

"Then you'd better eat up," says Mum. "You've no time to lose." She turns her attention to Short-Stuff who is flat out dive-bombing the floor with her dinner. All around her high chair looks like a battle zone.

I put my head down and glare at my dinner. How can you talk to your teacher with a stomach full of horrible meatballs? What a rotten day. Right from when the new girl started.

Miss Soames is really excited when I tell her about Wangs and the computer. She tells me it doesn't matter about the bread factory. It can be a treat for the most deserving class. So the computer will go to the class who makes the most money, and the trip to the bread factory will go to the class who tries the hardest, but doesn't win.

When I hear that, my heart sinks lower than my full stomach. I bet I know who that'll be. I told you our class was doomed.

Just as I'm handing the receiver over to Mum so she can explain every last detail to Miss Soames, I can hear a loud knocking coming from the door.

I go and open it. Joel is standing there.

"Hi," he says, like everything is normal. "Do you want to go for a training walk?"

I can see that Joel is still sick. But I decide to ignore it. "Mum," I yell. "Can I go for a walk with Joel?"

Mum puts her hand over the mouthpiece. "I thought you had a lot of homework."

I grin and look sheepish.

Mum shakes her head. "All right. But no longer than half an hour." Then, before I can make a move, the day gets worse. Mum adds, "Be a dear and take Stephanie with you."

Oh, great. That means I have to stay on the footpath right in front of the house so Mum can hear Short-Stuff if she screams or something. I want to try and get things

33

straightened out between Joel and me. And now how can I?

It's still daylight outside and warm, even though it's 7.30 p.m. The sun is making streamers down our street. It's really nice. In summer, this is the best time of the day.

We walk down the driveway. Short-Stuff is gurgling and goo-gooing to herself in her pushchair. I open my mouth to tell Joel about the computer, then guess who comes around the corner? Duana. It's like she's got an antenna on the two of us. Or is it just Joel? Before she can start hypnotizing Joel again, she notices Short-Stuff.

"Oh," she says, kneeling down beside the pushchair. "What a cutie." And that's enough for Short-Stuff. She loves someone making a fuss of her. She starts tugging at her socks and showing off. Then something happens. Duana starts speaking in a strange language.

"Ooos a bootiful baby. Iggie. Wiggie. Bootiful baby."

Joel and I look away. It's too embarrassing! But Short-Stuff loves it. She gurgles and chuckles at the attention.

"Ibble-dibble doo."

I cringe. It's getting out of hand. If Mum could hear Duana talking baby talk, she'd go nuts. She says you've got to use proper words when you're talking to babies.

"Got to get moving," I say in a loud voice.

Duana stands up. "Oh, are you going somewhere special?"

"We're training for the walk-a-thon," blurts out Joel.

No need to tell you what happens next. Duana ends up walking with us. We walk back and forth with Duana talking the whole time. She tells us she is staying at her grandmother's house, which is on Wilbur Street, the street next to Joel's and mine (wouldn't you know it) until her parents come back from overseas in three weeks' time.

By the time I get home, it's pretty late. Short-Stuff is asleep in the pushchair. Mum is mad and upset, thinking something awful has happened to us. But nothing has. Except for one thing. I discover how much fun Duana is and how much I like her.

Chapter 5

The next morning, I get up early. At least it's early for me. Usually I lie scrunched under the covers until Dad comes and pulls them off. But before I went to sleep last night, I made two resolutions:

1. I'm going to get into shape. So in shape that Duana will be sorry she didn't ask me to be her partner on the walk-a-thon.

2. I'm going to get the most names on my sponsor card, and then if I walk the furthest and have the most names, our class will have a good chance of winning the computer.

In my daydream, I can already see the tears of happiness in Miss Soames's eyes and feel her strong arm around my skinny shoulders. She's calling me a champion. Duana and Joel are hanging around, envious. "That'll teach the two of them," I think as I go into the kitchen.

Dad is up already, yawning and making a cup of tea. His eyes flick towards the clock.

"It's OK, Dad. I decided to get up early," I say quickly, stopping any frantic calls to the doctor in case he's thinking I might be sick.

"What's the occasion?" he asks.

"I'm going for a jog."

"What!" exclaims Dad as though it's the last thing I'd ever think of doing. Yesterday morning, he'd have been right.

"I'm going to get into shape for Pine Trail."

Dad pours hot water into two cups then turns and grins at me. "How come you're going for a jog when it's a walk-a-thon?"

I take no notice of his teasing. Instead I ask, "Did you hear about the computer?"

"I sure did. Great, eh?"

"It will be, if our class gets it," I say.

Dad lifts out the soggy tea bags and drops them into the sink.

I head towards the back door. "Can you tell Mum where I've gone?" I say, stepping outside quickly, in case he makes me go and tell her myself. Sometimes Mum worries too much about what I'm up to. I close the door quietly behind me.

The morning is cool; the sun is up but still hidden behind the houses. The only other time I've ever been up this early was when Short-Stuff was born. Dad woke me up at 5.30 in the morning, and then the three of us drove down the dark city streets until we got to the hospital.

The hospital is a long way from where we live. Then, wouldn't you know it, after all that rushing, Short-Stuff decides not to be born until the afternoon. The next day at school, Miss Soames makes me give a talk about it. She loves it when something different has happened and always likes us to share it with the class.

By the end of the street, I'm totally out of breath. If I can't even jog this little way, how am I going to be able to do the walk-a-thon without collapsing? I decide to try walking fast instead of jogging.

By the end of another block, my legs are aching and my throat is dry. Maybe it'd be easier if I crawl? I sigh and struggle on, my steps getting slower and slower. Where's the champion I dreamed of? Ha! More like a champion dreamer.

I turn around and head back home. I take it slowly, giving myself time to breathe.

There's no way I'm giving up. Not with a computer in the offering. Room Three is going to have to fight to win this one.

When I get home, I stagger into the kitchen and head straight for the cold water.

"How did it go?" asks Dad when I rush past him.

"Can't talk," I gasp. I turn on the water and stick my mouth under it. After I've had a big drink, I feel better.

"I take it your jog went OK then," says Dad, chuckling.

Mum comes in carrying Short-Stuff. "I'm really proud of you, Matt," she says, sliding Short-Stuff into the high chair. "Dad told me about your training programme for the walk." She leans over and kisses the top of my head.

I manage a feeble grin. If only she knew why I was really doing it.

"Of course the computer wouldn't have anything to do with it. Would it?" asks Dad.

I shake my head and look out the window so they can't see my guilty face. At least it's not a total lie. Just a half one. Then I burst out laughing. I can't help it. Down in the street is the funniest thing I've ever seen.

"What's so hilarious?" says Dad, coming over.

Joel is all decked out in his best shorts, T-shirt, and sneakers, striding down the street, swinging his arms. He looks like a soldier with wooden arms and legs.

Dad grins when he sees Joel, then he gives me a puzzled look. "How come the pair of you didn't go together? I've never known you to do anything without each other." He gazes at me. "Are you two fighting about something?"

I turn away from the window. "I only just decided this morning, Dad. I haven't had time to talk to Joel about it." I know I don't sound very convincing, but I'm not going into all the explanation about Duana. It would sound too pathetic.

Before Dad can ask me any in-depth questions, Short-Stuff bangs her spoon on the tray of her high chair, demanding her breakfast.

I let out a silent sigh of relief. But then it hits me. Joel's obviously got the same idea as me. Even when we do things separately, we end up doing the same thing. Then I wonder what Joel is walking for. Is it for Duana or the computer? But the thought has no sooner entered my head, than I know it has to be Duana. Why? Simple! Joel doesn't know about the computer yet. And if that's the case, then I guess he's heading to be my worst enemy, instead of my best friend. And it's all because of Miss Soames's wild walking idea and Duana O'Neill.

Later, after I've had breakfast, packed my backpack, and said goodbye to Mum, Dad, and Short-Stuff, I set off for school. On the way, as usual, I call in at Joel's house. He's waiting for me, which is a bit of a change. Usually, I have to wait ages while he gets ready. While walking to school, I wait for him to say something about his early-morning walk. I've decided that if he tells me, then I'll tell him about my training programme. I think that's fair. After all, I'm not the one who's doing the deserting.

Joel doesn't mention it.

I push down the hurt feelings creeping around inside me. Then I notice him limping. He must have done something to his leg on his secret walk.

"What happened to your leg?"

"Nothing," he says.

I stay silent, giving him every chance to explain, but he keeps his mouth shut. Instead, he changes the subject and starts to talk about his latest invention. An invention that takes the shells off hard-boiled eggs. Before he gets out more than five words, I interrupt him.

"I thought you said you weren't allowed to make any more inventions. That you're banned from your dad's tools."

Joel makes a face. "Dad keeps forgetting. But I might as well be."

"Why?"

"Mum's really mad at me."

"Why?" I ask, sounding like my own echo.

Joel sighs. "I boiled all the eggs so I could test my new invention…"

"And?"

"The eggs had pieces of shell stuck in them. Mum had to throw them all out."

All the time he's going on about his shell shedder, I'm dying to tell him about Wangs and the Black Arrow computer. When there's a moment of silence, I open my mouth to tell him, but I'm stopped in my tracks by the sound of a familiar voice calling from behind.

"Wait up, Joel."

Duana!

As much as I like her, she is starting to get on my nerves. There never seems to be any place she doesn't turn up at. Talk about taking up all the space between Joel and me. I wish she'd never come to our school. And to think it was only yesterday. It seems like she's been around forever.

Joel doesn't look at me. He keeps his face down as though he's studying the weeds growing through the cracks in the footpath.

Duana catches us up. "I stopped by your house," she says to Joel.

This is getting serious. Am I ever going to be able to talk to Joel on his own again? Duana's getting to be like a jack-in-the-box. Popping up unexpectedly all the time. This thought makes me mad. I start to walk fast. Then faster and faster until I'm running. Running far away from Duana and Joel. But all the time I'm waiting for Joel to shout out to wait for him. But he doesn't.

When I reach the school gates, I look back. Duana and Joel are still at the end of the street, dawdling and chatting. Like they belong together. So where does that leave me?

I turn around and plod through the school gates on my own. Sometimes things aren't fair. Not fair at all.

Chapter 6

Of course I should have known Miss Soames would make me tell the class about Wangs and the computer. I'm on my way to my desk when Miss Soames swoops down on me and gives me a tremendous hug. I think my shoulder cracked.

After I've explained the little bit there is to explain, Miss Soames takes over.

"Isn't that wonderful?" she says, her enthusiasm filling the room. "Let's give a big round of applause for Matt."

I go back to my seat, her words ringing sweet in my ears, "a big round of applause for Matt... a big round of applause for Matt..." until I see Joel's red and furious face. I turn away, pretending I haven't noticed. Well, I would have told him about the computer if he hadn't been so busy with Duana. I haven't had the chance. Not really.

"Now," says Miss Soames, "this latest news calls for a real effort from all of us. After all, think of how much benefit and fun a computer would be. It's not every day that a chance like this comes along."

Tracy puts up her hand. "I've got three names on my card, Miss Soames."

"Good, Tracy. I can see you're off to a flying start."

Miss Soames looks around the room. "Anyone else?"

Silence.

"What? No one at all?" Miss Soames pulls her little lips together while her eyes search and probe around the room in case she's missed someone.

I stick up my hand. I'm not sure why, I think it's probably something to do with being determined to try and get the other kids in the class to take the walk-a-thon seriously. Try to make them see we've got just as much chance as Room Three of winning the computer. And that we can't give in without a fight. I'm sure Joel will be thinking the same thing. After all, he's computer mad, especially when it comes to the Black Arrow. At least, he was up until yesterday. But today, who knows? Look at the way he's changed his mind about walking.

"Matt?" says Miss Soames.

"Dad says he's going to sign my card tonight."

Miss Soames nods. "Yes. Grand."

After that, Miss Soames asks Duana to tell us about herself.

Duana gets up and goes to the front of the class. The sun catches the side of her hair and makes it all shiny. She starts off by telling us about some of the places she's been to. I haven't even heard of some of them. She explains it's because both her parents are journalists and they have to travel all over the world on assignments.

"How exciting," murmurs Miss Soames.

"Sometimes it's really great," says Duana, then her smile fades. "But most of the time I don't get to go with them. Often it's too dangerous. Instead, I usually stay with a family from a childcare agency."

How awful! Being shoved around to stay with different people all the time. I can't even imagine life without Mum, Dad, and Short-Stuff. And Marla.

Miss Soames's voice cuts through my thoughts. "So there's just you, Duana? No brothers or sisters?"

Duana bites the side of her lip. "I had a little brother, but he died... I don't know what happened... it was... it was a long time ago now," she says in a big rush.

After hearing that, I wish Miss Soames hadn't asked Duana to tell us about her life. How can I be angry with her now for butting in between Joel and me, knowing what happened to her brother? And knowing about her never having a real home. Always living with strangers.

Miss Soames nods, waits for a second, then asks Duana if she would finish up by sharing her hobbies with the class. Before Duana can reply, there's a knock on the door. Mr Good, Room Three's teacher, opens the door and hovers with one foot in our room as though he's scared something might bite him. He motions to Miss Soames.

Miss Soames walks over to the door. "Carry on," she says to Duana, closing the door behind her. I'm half-listening to Duana but at the same time I'm also trying to listen to what Mr Good and Miss Soames are talking about out in the corridor. When teachers talk outside the classroom, it's usually something important. Something they don't want us to know about until they're ready.

Two minutes later, Miss Soames comes back into the room. Duana is telling us about the certificates she's won in gymnastics. She's never stayed at one school long enough to get a chance at winning a championship cup.

When we've given Duana a round of applause for her talk, Miss Soames holds up her hand. Her face looks sad. It must have to do with what Mr Good wanted to talk to her about.

"Unfortunately," starts off Miss Soames, "it seems that Duana is no longer going to be staying with us."

Duana looks startled.

"Nothing's happened to your parents," says Miss Soames, guessing what Duana is thinking. "No. It seems you should have been in Room Three all along."

Talk about feeling devastated! Duana is too smart for us. In other words, she's brainy just like the Room Three kids. Miss Soames says there's no difference between Room Three and us, but I know there is. Suddenly I feel everything is hopeless. Again our class is going down the drain. Why does Room Three always get everything that is halfway decent?

"But you can't go into Room Three," exclaims Tracy, gazing at Duana, tears in her eyes. "They're horrible."

And for once, I agree with Tracy.

I glance over at Joel, wondering what he's thinking. He's staring straight ahead.

Everyone starts talking at once. Soon the classroom is buzzing like angry bees while my head is going around in circles. One minute I can't stand Duana, the next minute I like her.

What's going on? Surely I should be glad Duana's going to Room Three. If she does, it'll mean Joel can't be her partner in the walk-a-thon. He can be mine instead. So why don't I want her to leave our class? Why do I feel Duana is one of us?

Then, before I can stop myself, I find my arm going up, my hand waving around in the air, and my voice calling out, "Excuse me, Miss Soames."

Miss Soames claps her hands several times. Finally the racket stops. "Yes, Matt, what is it?"

"Couldn't we have a protest?" I say, not really believing it's me saying it.

"What kind of protest?" Miss Soames looks slightly puzzled.

"A protest about Duana going to Room Three," I explain. "We could get the whole class to sign it and then take it to Ms Dingle." I slump back in my chair, exhausted by my effort. I still feel mixed-up inside, knowing that if the protest works, and Ms Dingle (she's the principal) lets Duana stay in our class, that'll be the end of Joel and me being walking partners.

Noise fills the classroom again, but this time it's filled with excitement. Miss Soames holds up her hands. Quiet falls.

"All right!" she says, "I can see that Duana is quite a hit with you all." She looks over at Duana. "But perhaps before we start running off to Ms Dingle with all sorts of protests, I think we should find out what Duana wants."

The whole class stares at Duana.

"Well, Duana?" encourages Miss Soames.

Duana clasps her hands tightly together. She opens her mouth and speaks slowly. "I think this class is the best ever," she says, blinking hard.

"I take that as a 'yes' then," says Miss Soames, smiling. "That you're happy to stay here rather than go to Room Three?"

Duana nods fiercely.

We all cheer. Somehow it feels like we've won our first battle against Room Three. Joel turns to me and puts up both his thumbs. I grin until it covers my face like a rash. What does it matter if we don't do the walk together? What does it matter if Duana is his partner instead of me? Nah! It doesn't. What really matters is Joel and me being friends.

Chapter 7

In the end, our class doesn't have to do a protest to stop Duana going into Room Three. Miss Soames and Duana go to see Ms Dingle themselves, and when they return to the classroom, they are both smiling. Tracy rushes up to Duana and guides her back to her seat like she's a TV star.

"It seems that so long as Duana is happy where she is," says Miss Soames, "then she can stay."

Hurray! For the rest of the time before morning break, I don't bother paying much attention to the maths lesson. Instead, my mind is thinking about the walk. Now that we've won something against Room Three, what's to stop us from winning again? I ignore the fact that the Room Three kids never had a clue that Duana should have been in their class. I can't help feeling good about it.

By morning break, I've got a plan. A plan that might just get us to win the walk-a-thon.

But I'll need help. Especially from Joel. So as soon as the bell goes, I rush up to him and start by apologizing.

"I'm sorry I didn't tell you about the computer, but I was mad at you. And it's OK if you want Duana for your partner."

Joel turns and shakes his head. "It wasn't you being stupid. It was me."

"No," I insist. "It was me."

"Sometimes I'm such an idiot," says Joel, not listening to me. "I'm sorry, Matt."

"Yeah. OK," I say, giving in, realizing that if I don't let him apologize, he could go on all day and night. Besides, I'm desperate to tell him about my plan and see what he thinks. "Hey! Listen. I've had this idea about the walk-a-thon."

"Imagine," Joel sighs. "A brand new Black Arrow computer!"

At that moment, Duana runs over, closely followed by Tracy. She stops in front of me.

"Thanks, Matt, for doing what you did."

"What?" I'm embarrassed.

"I've never had anyone want to set up a protest to keep me. Usually it's the other way around."

I laugh nervously. Before her morning talk, I'd been thinking exactly that! "It was nothing," I mumble, then quickly change the subject. "What chance do you think we have of winning the walk?"

"As good as Room Three," replies Duana.

"You're kidding!" exclaims Tracy.

The next minute, there's a noise like thunder booming behind us. The four of us swing around. But it's not a storm coming. It's Room Three pounding toward us, arms swinging and legs whirling, on their great practice walk.

"Do you think we can beat that?" says Joel, his voice filling with despair.

"It's easy to walk fast on flat ground," says Duana.

Easy? I grimace, remembering how I felt on my walk this morning. As Room Three passes us, one of them calls out, "Thanks for the computer, Matt."

That makes my blood boil.

"Hear that?" says Tracy, gawking at me.

"You don't have it yet," I yell, trying to make myself feel better. It doesn't. Deep down my one bubble of hope bursts.

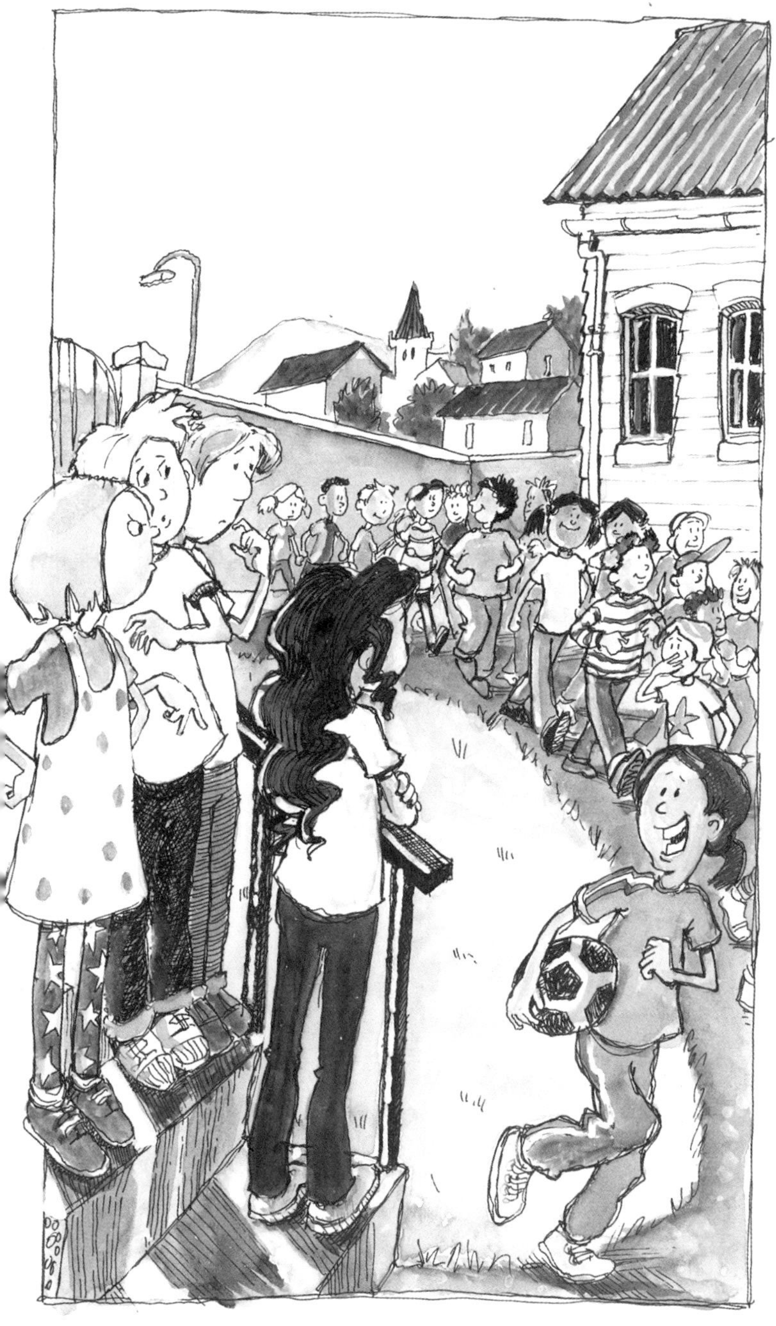

When Room Three have marched out of sight, Joel turns to me. "So what's your idea?"

"It sounds dumb now," I say.

"It's got to be better than nothing. And that's what we're going to have if we don't do something."

Joel glares at me for a long time. He suddenly looks determined. A look I've only seen once before. He hadn't been at the school long when our class went swimming. And, like I've said, Joel is hopeless at sports. Some kids started to tease him about what a terrible swimmer he was. They were saying that a plastic duck could do way better than Joel. Well that did it. The next minute, Joel jumps in at the shallow end and tries to swim all the way to the deep end. He got really puffed and started sinking. The teacher had to jump in and pull him out. But you've got to hand it to Joel, he wasn't going to let those kids put him down. I suppose now with a Black Arrow computer in sight, it's the same sort of thing. He's not going to give in without a fight.

"Tell us. Please," urges Duana.

"Yeah," echoes Tracy. "Tell us, Matt."

I clear my throat, then start off slowly. "It's like this. The class that gets in the most sponsorship money gets the computer, right?"

The three of them nod.

"So to win, all we've got to do is find someone who is really rich and has millions to give away."

"How come?" asks Tracy, her brown eyes staring right into my face.

I sigh. "Look! Say your mum gives you a little bit of money a kilometre, then you're going to have to walk forever to make any money. But if your mum gives you lots of money a kilometre, then you're going to make a lot more walking the same distance."

"If you're trying to say my mum's stingy, Matt, you're wrong!"

"I never said…" I start, then let it drop.

"Yeah," says Joel, nodding his head like a puppet. "You're right." Then he frowns. "But no one around here has lots of money."

"I told you it was hopeless."

"Wait!" exclaims Duana, smiling. "There might be a way."

We crowd closer, waiting to hear her magic answer.

"Can we get sponsors from anywhere?" Duana asks.

"I don't know," I say. "Why?" Knowing that even if I knew a hundred people on the other side of the world, it wouldn't make any difference. None of them would have any money.

"Just because…" says Duana mysteriously. The school bell puts an end to our discussion. Going back to the classroom, Duana pulls me to one side. "Matt," she whispers, "see if you can get Miss Soames to explain more about the sponsors."

"You mean find out if they have to come from around here?"

Duana nods. "Yeah. And…"

Joel interrupts. "I've been working on some supersonic sneakers," he says in a hushed voice. "They might come in handy."

I stifle a giggle. Knowing the history of Joel's inventions, they'll most likely end up making him walk backwards or something just as crazy.

"I can test them for you," Tracy breathes over Joel's shoulder. Joel pretends not to hear and rushes quickly to his seat.

Duana nudges me. "Don't forget to ask about the sponsors, Matt. Make it casual." Then she zips over to her desk as Miss Soames enters the room.

It's not until after lunch that I get a chance to ask Miss Soames about the walking sponsors. For the rest of the morning, we are too busy making a cool paper mâché mobile of the solar system. There was no way I was even thinking about the walk with something so fantastically interesting happening.

But then Miss Soames goes straight into our spelling lesson. So before she can get started on the list of words on the whiteboard, I put up my hand to ask about the sponsors.

"Miss Soames, I was wondering…" I stop, not sure what to say next. Good one, Matt!

Miss Soames turns her attention towards me. "Yes, Matt?"

"Is it all right to get Marla to sign my card?" I ask, saying the first thing that pops into my head.

61

Miss Soames looks puzzled.

"As a sponsor for the walk," I add, getting up more confidence. "Marla, my sister, doesn't live around here. Most of the time she's in a forest." I'm thinking that if it's OK for her to sign my card and give money to the walk, then it'd be OK if the person lived on the moon.

"Matt! What a good question. Thank you." Miss Soames smiles at me, her little lips stretching out as far as they can go. "How refreshing to know there is someone who is genuinely interested in trying to help."

Hearing that, I feel more slippery than a polished floor. If only she knew the truth! All I really care about is beating Room Three. It's a good thing no one can empty out our heads at the end of the day and see what we've been thinking.

Miss Soames's happy voice interrupts my wild thoughts. "As the object of the project is to make money – money that will help other children – then any sponsor is welcome. Even if they come from the furthest corner of the earth." At that, Miss Soames gives a huge laugh as though that's the most impossible thing that could happen.

When Miss Soames goes back to the whiteboard to add a few more spelling words, I look over at Duana. She winks and grins. Tracy waves, and Joel turns and wiggles his eyebrows. Idiots!

After school, the four of us dawdle down the street together.

"How about we really get into this walking thing?" says Duana.

"You mean training and stuff like that?"

"Yeah, and what we were talking about before." Duana lowers her voice and gives a furtive look over her shoulder. "Look, we can't talk here. You never know where the enemy is. They might have spies."

Tracy's eyes open wide. "Enemy? Spies?"

"Room Three," says Joel, glaring at her, making it obvious he's sorry she's in with us. But it's too late to do anything about Tracy now. Joel will just have to put up with her. Besides, you never know, she might even be some help.

"Oh them!" Tracy lets out her breath. "They couldn't even climb a tree."

Sometimes when Tracy speaks it's like listening to someone from another galaxy.

"We need to have a meeting," says Duana.

"I guess we could have it at my place after dinner," I volunteer, ignoring the red warning signals in my head. I know it'll be mayhem at my house – with Short-Stuff not wanting to go to bed, Dad singing to her, and Mum making millions of phone calls.

"I could do some drawings," says Tracy.

Duana, Joel, and I stop talking. We turn and stare at Tracy.

"I'm good at cats," she adds.

What is she going on about? Even someone from a different galaxy would have trouble understanding this one.

Joel opens his mouth and starts to speak very slowly, forcing himself to stay calm. "What does drawing cats have to do with the walk?"

"I'll tell you at the meeting tonight," says Tracy. Then she runs off down the street, and before any of us can utter a word, she's turned the corner and gone.

Chapter 8

When Mum and Dad get home, they're both in a bad mood. I don't know what about and I don't ask. Short-Stuff is whining and trying to gnaw at my hand when I put her in the high chair. Mum tells me Short-Stuff is teething. I decide not to mention the meeting. Instead I check out an idea I've had.

"Dad, is Mr Wang rich?" I ask, while helping peel some potatoes. My peeling isn't very good. By the time I've finished, my potatoes look like marbles.

"He's got money, all right." Dad drops a potato into the pot, splashing water all over the sink. "Too much! That's the problem."

How can too much money be a problem?

Dad leans on the bench and stares out the window. "Do you know what he's thinking of doing, Matt?"

I shake my head.

"He's thinking of opening another Wangs."

"Wow! He really must be rich." Mental

visions of Mr Wang signing my sponsor card float before my eyes. Go ahead and walk your legs off, Room Three!

"Sounds good, eh?" says Dad, jerking himself back to the potatoes and stabbing at one. "And guess who he wants to run it?"

It doesn't take me long to get it. "Mum?"

Dad nods. "You got it in one, Matt."

I frown, not sure why he sounds so upset. Surely if Mum is the manager of a Wangs Supermarket, it can only be good for us. "Doesn't Mum want to?" I ask.

"Oh, she wants to, all right."

I put another marble potato into the pot and wait for Dad to explain.

"The trouble is," sighs Dad, "he's thinking of opening it in Finslow."

I gasp, beginning to understand.

Dad and I finish peeling the potatoes in silence. Dad loves living in Wansborough. He's lived here all his life. Mum comes from a big city up north.

One time, we almost moved. But in the end, Mum didn't get the job she was after, so it didn't happen. But now? Mum will never turn down this.

Dad breaks the silence. "So, Matt, what do you say to leaving Wansborough?"

"No way," I protest, not daring to think of life without Joel on my doorstep. But suddenly, I realize how Duana must feel every time she has to move. "I like it here, Dad."

"Me too, Matt. Me too."

The meeting gets off to a rough start. I do try to tell Mum about it, but every time I open my mouth to explain, she gives me another job to do. She has this habit of giving me lots to do when she's in a bad mood. That seems to be her best cure.

Anyway, before I've finished emptying the rubbish bin, Joel and Duana arrive. Mum raises her eyebrows.

"We're having this meeting about the walk-a-thon," I gabble quickly.

"What about your homework?" she asks.

It's weird the way Mum worries about my homework all the time. The way she goes on, you'd think I was studying to be a brain surgeon. "I've only got a few spelling words to learn," I tell her.

When Dad comes into the kitchen carrying Short-Stuff, I suddenly realize things could get really ugly if Duana starts talking baby talk. Mum is too grumpy to handle it. The meeting would be over before it got started.

"Hi, kids. What's happening?" says Dad, looking at Duana and putting an invisible question mark over her head.

"This is Duana," I tell Mum and Dad. "She's been in our class since Monday. She's staying with her grandmother."

Duana smiles at them both and says, "It's nice of you to let us have the meeting here."

"We'd better get started," I say, my instincts warning me again to keep Duana away from Short-Stuff, with the mood Mum's in.

Mum forces a smile, and Dad asks Duana where her grandmother lives. While I listen to Duana, I realize she is quite cunning. Not a mean cunning, but a clever cunning. A cunning that gets them to like her so that they're on her side right from the start.

Short-Stuff starts to squeal. Duana stops talking and tickles her hand.

Uh-oh!

"Woos such a booti..." begins Duana, goo-gooing.

I interrupt her with a loud spluttering cough, nearly choking myself. At least my sudden convulsion stops Duana in her tracks, and before she can start again, there's a loud knock at the door.

Mum turns to me. "How many others are coming?" she asks.

"No more," I say, letting Tracy in. She is carrying a large drawing pad and some felt-tip pens.

Then before Duana can open her mouth again, I quickly hurry her, Joel, and Tracy in the direction of my room. And at the same time, I'm making desperate promises to help Mum when Marla and her boyfriend come this weekend. I shut my bedroom door.

"Sorry. But my mum's in a bad mood," I explain.

"Your mum is nice," says Tracy.

"Yeah. Usually."

The meeting starts with Duana telling us all about this woman who owns five fish factories. "I stayed with her for eight months when we were in Argentina," she explains. "She's got the most amazing place…"

"Imagine that," mutters Tracy. "Five fish factories."

Duana continues. "Brunella Lala, that's her name, has got piles of money. And before I left, she told me that if there was ever anything she could do for me, I only had to let her know."

"But how's that going to help us?" says Joel.

"She could be one of my sponsors," says Duana, smiling.

Joel gives a little "hmm," then says, "But don't you remember Miss Soames telling us that all sponsor cards have to be signed by the sponsor; otherwise, they'll be no good? There's not much time left."

Duana laughs. "Haven't you lot heard of a fax machine?"

"Of course we have," says Joel crossly.

"I'd like to see a real one," says Tracy, wide-eyed.

I stifle a grin. Poor Tracy. All machines are real. But I suppose she means one that's not on TV.

"I'll show you Gran's sometime," says Duana. "My dad bought it for her. So what do you think?"

There's a small silence. Then Joel says, "I'd really love to see the fax machine, too."

"Duana wasn't talking about that..." I shake my head. This meeting is getting right off the walking trail. I snigger to myself. That's a good one. Off the walking trail! And that's where we'll be unless we get a move on.

"I think it's a brilliant idea," I say, writing it down on the sheet of paper with the heading "Brilliant Ideas for the Walk-a-thon".

"Do you want to hear my idea?" Tracy asks hopefully, gazing at the three of us. She puts her drawing pad down in front of us.

"As long as it doesn't take too long," comments Joel, narrowing his eyes.

Tracy opens her drawing pad. We lean over to look. "See, it's a map of Pine Trail," she explains. "And that's our class." She points to figures, drawn in different-coloured felt-tip pens, on different parts of the trail.

I'm totally amazed, and I can see Joel is as well. I never knew Tracy could even draw a straight line, let alone something as good as this. The page is headed "Kids Saving Kids". All around the map are drawings of lots of different children. Along the bottom is a chart showing the things the money we raise can be used for: food, drinking water, blankets, clothes, and lots of other stuff. "Dad helped me with that part," admits Tracy.

"Did you draw all this on your own?" asks Duana, a note of wonder in her voice.

Tracy nods. "It's my secret hobby," she whispers. "I've never shown anyone my drawings before." She looks at us shyly. "I didn't want anyone to laugh."

Joel looks uncomfortable and squirms on the floor as though there's some bubblegum stuck to the bottom of his jeans.

"What about the cats?" I ask, knowing it's a stupid question, but it's out before I can stop myself. Seeing what Tracy's done has really impressed me and I can't seem to think straight.

Tracy giggles. "That was a trick. It's just that I draw cats best of all."

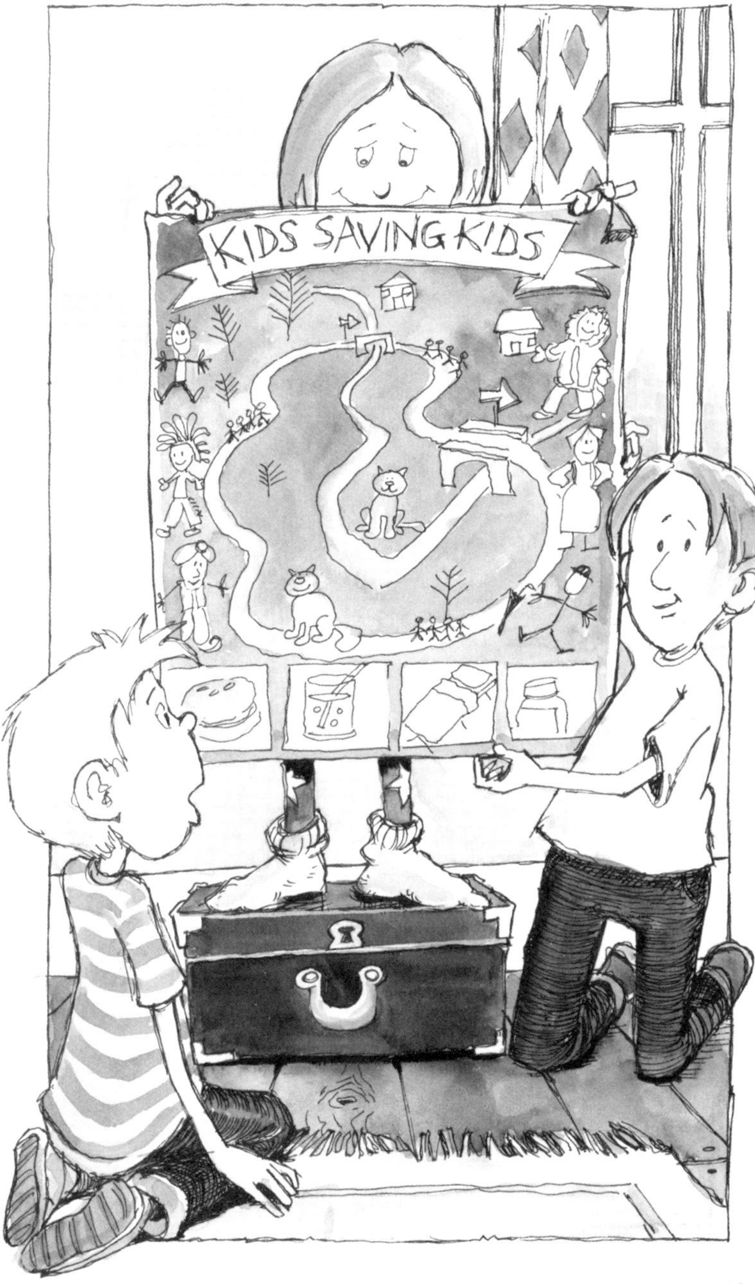
KIDS SAVING KIDS

"I think your drawing is excellent," says Joel in a thoughtful voice. "But how's it going to help with the walk?"

Tracy explains. "If we can get some copies done, then we can show it to people. It might make them more interested in sponsoring us."

"Right. An advertising blast!" says Duana. "Great stuff!"

I write Tracy's idea down on my sheet of paper. So far two brilliant ideas. Beating Room Three is beginning to seem possible.

"Yeah!" exclaims Joel, showing definite signs of excitement. "And then we could stick them all over the place, telling everyone to support our class."

Duana shakes her head. "No! Do you want Room Three to know what we're up to and copy us?"

"But I still haven't worked out where we can get copies done for nothing," says Tracy, sighing. "Do you know of anywhere?"

"How about Mr Doon in the library?" suggests Joel.

I shake my head. "He'll make us pay. Don't you remember all the fuss he made over Miss Soames and the school fair?"

Another silence. Then it hits me. "I know. Mum has a photocopier at work. I think they may even have a fax machine. But there's no way I'm asking her tonight. I'll wait until she's in a better mood." I write, "Ask Mum about getting copies done". Then I turn to Tracy and tell her I'll need the drawing.

"You won't let anything happen to it?"

"Of course not." I make a mental note to put it up high, far away from Short-Stuff's busy hands.

When the business of Tracy's poster and copies are finished, Duana says, "How about we do some serious training for the walk?"

"We could do that before school, then afterwards, we could go out to collect sponsors," says Joel.

"Hang on," I say. "Does everyone agree about the training first?"

Three heads nod.

"All right. Then it's 8.00 a.m. outside Joel's place. And everyone has to be on time. Agreed?"

Again, three heads nod.

"And what about us collecting sponsors after school?"

Nod. Nod. Nod.

I give a private shudder. Already I can hear Mum's voice going on about my homework. But it can't be helped. This is a good cause and she knows it.

At that moment, the door opens a crack and Dad pokes his head around. "Anyone for a snack?"

The next second, my bedroom is empty except for me. I'm still writing stuff down. When I've finished, I look at the list. At least now I think we've got more of a chance of doing a good job of the walk-a-thon. We may be able to raise heaps of money for the kids who had that flood. And maybe they'll be even better off than they were before the flood. That would be really cool.

Chapter 9

By Saturday morning, several things have happened. I'm lying on my bed thinking about them. Some are definitely A+, some not.

1. Wangs put up posters about the Save-the-Kids Walk-a-thon. Everywhere. Big coloured ones. They look fantastic! A+

2. There was a big spread in the local paper about the event and how Wangs was donating a computer. Plus a photograph of Miss Soames explaining about it. She had a big smile on her little lips, while one arm was crushing the shoulders of Meredith Turpine who had just broken her leg and wouldn't be able to go on the walk. Cunning Meredith. A+ for Miss Soames. B- for Meredith.

3. Mum said I could do as many copies of Tracy's drawing as I wanted on the photocopier at work. She said she'd pay for them as part of her contribution towards the project. She also told Tracy she had a real talent and asked if she would like to

do a mural on one of the walls in the supermarket's crèche. Tracy was thrilled. A+ to Mum.

4. Joel finished his supersonic sneakers (a pair of old sneakers with springs). But they were a bit of a dud. After putting them on, he gave a small jump to get his feet started, and he couldn't stop. Then boing! boing! Away he went down the street like a jumping bean, only stopping when he shot into a hedge. The training that morning was hopeless. Duana, Tracy, and I couldn't stop laughing. Joel was mad at first, but he came around after a while. Definitely A+++

5. Duana sent a fax to Brunella Lala, the fish-factory lady in Argentina (we all watched), but her secretary replied saying she was off somewhere taking a break and she didn't know where she was. So unless Brunella gets back very soon, that's Duana's brilliant sponsor down the drain. B-

6. Mum told me about how Wangs might be opening another supermarket in Finslow and she could be the manager. She told me nothing was definite yet, but if it does go ahead, then she would take the position. F

7. Short-Stuff got another tooth and very nearly bit off Dad's finger. A+ for Short-Stuff. B- for Dad's finger.

8. The training programme is going OK. Tracy is always late and she walks so slowly. We tell her to hurry, but she takes no notice. Maybe it has something to do with being good at drawing. B-

9. So far, between the four of us, we've got sixty-eight sponsors. Tracy's poster has helped a lot. I've got fifteen, Duana has seventeen, and Joel's got eleven (he says he's been too busy trying to fix the supersonic sneakers). Tracy's got twenty-five. A++

10. Marla called on Friday to say she won't be coming this weekend after all. Her boyfriend won a trip for two to Moon Beach and so they're off there instead. It's a real downer. I was wanting Marla to get heaps of forestry workers to sign my sponsor card. C-

After thinking about all these things, I roll over on my bed and stare at the ceiling. If only our class could beat Room Three and make millions. Then, if Wangs does build a new supermarket in Finslow and we do leave Wansborough, at least I will have helped to make our class famous. We might even go down in the school's history books. I'm so busy thinking about my space-age dreams, I don't notice my bedroom door opening. Then I see Joel standing next to my bed.

I sit up with a jerk. "What's happening?" I ask.

He sighs. "It's all over," he says, his face longer than the longest night in the middle of winter.

"What's over?"

"I'm not ever allowed to invent anything ever again."

"Uh-oh!"

"It wasn't my fault. Not really," he says, staring glumly at the floor.

"Tell me."

He lets out a desperate sigh. "Well... I broke the TV."

"Wow!"

"Yeah!"

I'm dying to ask how, but I know it's best to let Joel tell me when he's ready.

"It's all because of the stupid walk," Joel says. "I'd just finished fixing up the sneakers with the springs. It took me ages, but they worked really well." He pauses and swallows. "I was testing them out in the living room. Everything was going fine until my mum suddenly shouts that I should test them outside. That's when it happens." He pauses.

"Yeah…"

"My foot lands on one of Kyla's stupid roller skates. The next thing I know, I'm flying through the air. Then POW! I crash into the TV. The rest is history."

"What did your dad say?"

Joel makes a face. "He doesn't know. He's on the early shift."

For the rest of the day, I don't see Joel again. But when I take Short-Stuff for a walk on my way to meet Duana and Tracy, I see a notice stuck onto his window. It is written in big black letters:

Help! I'm a Prisnar!

I stand puzzled for a second, then realize that Joel's spelling has gone a bit haywire. If Miss Soames saw this, she'd have us spelling the word "prisoner" night and day!

I meet up with Duana and Tracy and tell them about Joel. They're sitting in the sun in Duana's grandmother's garden.

"How about a daring rescue?" says Duana, excitement flashing over her face.

"No way," I say. "You don't know his mum. It'd only make things worse."

Duana shrugs. "OK. If you say so." She leans towards Short-Stuff. "I wish I had a little sister."

"I could do a drawing of Stephanie for you," says Tracy, her voice hesitant and shy. "If you want."

Duana nods. "That'd be fantastic. Then I can take it with me when I..." she stops in mid-sentence.

A cold chill runs down the back of my neck. Surely Duana's not moving already. She's only been in Wansborough for a week. But something deep inside me knows it's the truth. "But what about the walk-a-thon?" I say, anger rising, then I blurt out, "It's not fair. Can't your parents just leave you in one place for once?"

"Don't be silly, Matt. She's not going yet," explains Tracy. "She means one day. Not right now. That's right, isn't it, Duana?"

"No. Matt's right."

At this, Tracy gives a squeak of anguish.

"My dad called last night." Duana stares at the ground for a moment then smiles. "It's not so bad. Except I'll miss you guys. Being here has been the best thing ever."

"It stinks," I tell her, not caring what she thinks of me. Somehow life won't be the same without Duana.

"At least this time," continues Duana, "we'll all be together for once. Dad told me Mum's been sick. So we're taking a holiday. Imagine! A whole month in Rhodes."

"Where's that?" asks Tracy.

"Some island near Greece."

"What about the walk?" I growl.

Duana shakes her head. "Sorry, Matt. I tried to explain to Dad, but he said he'd already booked a flight for this Friday."

The rest of the afternoon is a total drag. We go for our training walk, but it doesn't feel the same knowing Duana's not going to be doing the walk-a-thon with us.

On my way home, I think about Joel. A real friend would tell him about Duana leaving. A real friend would also tell him that his best friend might be leaving and going to live in Finslow. As I pass Joel's window, I see another notice:

> it's a Big Mistake!
> I'M INNOCINT!

Looking at that, I decide Joel's got enough problems of his own. I'll tell him about Duana later, when things are sorted out. And much, much later, I'll tell him about Wangs opening up a supermarket in Finslow.

Chapter 10

THE WALK-A-THON IS FINALLY OVER! It's Sunday, the day after the gruelling walk. Every bone in my body aches, so I'm not getting out of bed until lunchtime. I'm lying here remembering all the stuff that went on last week.

The first thing is that Joel didn't really break the TV. When his dad came home from work, he jiggled a few pieces at the back of the TV, and presto – Joel was set free. But he's had to promise that any future inventions will be invented outside.

"Outside!" he snorts. "I bet the person who invented TV never had to do it outside. What happens if it rains?"

"You could invent something to stop the rain," I say, grinning.

Joel gives me a withering look. "You'll be sorry when I'm rich and famous."

When I tell him about Duana, he doesn't say much; he just nods the way he always does when he's starting to think about a new invention.

Friday is a desperate day. Miss Soames nearly crushes Duana when saying goodbye. Our class gives her a big card with all our names on it. Tracy gives her a drawing of Short-Stuff. I give her a pencil with her initials on it (it took me three tries to carve them). And Joel gives – get this – his can crusher! After Duana's opened all these exciting presents, she looks around the class with a wobbly smile. "Thank you so much," she says, her voice all choked up. We give her three cheers. At that moment, I get something in my eye and it makes it water. I blink hard, but before I can get rid of it, Duana's gone.

The next thing that happens is the walk-a-thon. It turns out to be the hottest day all year. Joel brings everything under the sun with him: a torch (in case he's still walking after dark), a compass, some string, money, and a book.

A book! I don't ask. Instead I say, "Where's your lunch?"

Joel makes a face, dumps his backpack on our doorstep, and rushes back home.

Tracy turns up wearing a pair of ugly sunglasses, her mother's sunhat (she wasn't allowed to go unless she wore it), and carrying her drawing pad and pencils. It looked like she was going on a picnic.

We were sizzling with heat even before we got to Pine Trail. It was a good thing there was plenty of water and juice at different points along the walk. Mum arranged that. Lots of kids got too hot and had to stop, but there was no way Joel and I were giving up. Tracy decided to walk on her own and do drawings of the whole event so she could send them to Duana. I kept thinking about what Duana had said to us. "Fix your mind on one thing. Concentrate on that, and you won't notice the aches." She told us that was what she did in gymnastics competitions. So all the way up Pine Trail and all the way back, I kept seeing our class winning the computer. And all the time, Joel was beside me.

And did we win? I wish I could say yes. But we don't know yet. Miss Soames got so flustered, what with the heat, lots of kids not finishing the walk, and different classes starting at different times, she told everyone the results would be announced on Monday.

So there's still a chance.

When Miss Soames stands up at assembly on Monday morning, there's a dead silence like you've never ever heard before. She's holding an important-looking piece of paper.

"First I want to say how proud I am of all of you..."

Tell us who won!

"...and after doing a final tally of all the sponsor cards, it is obvious that you have all put in a lot of effort."

SO WHO WON? shouts the voice in my head.

"The Save-the-Kids Walk-a-thon raised nearly three times as much money as we had hoped for," announces Miss Soames, her little lips beaming.

At that, the whole school goes bananas. We yell and cheer and clap. And, instead of telling us to be quiet, the teachers clap and cheer, too! Wow! I never knew there was so much money around here.

Miss Soames holds up her hand. When quiet returns, she says, "Before I give the rest of the results, I must mention the fact that a very generous donation came from an anonymous sponsor in Argentina. So to whoever arranged this, I would like to say an extra heartfelt thanks."

Duana! Brunella Lala must have got in touch with her. Excellent!

Miss Soames gazes down at Joel, Tracy, and me and nods. I guess she knows. She continues, "Now for the moment you've all been waiting for."

We must have won the computer! With Brunella's donation added to all our other money, we must have! I cross my fingers.

"The Black Arrow computer goes to Room Five, who raised the most money."

What? They're only little kids. I turn to Joel, but he's intently studying the floor. I feel weak, as though someone's knocked all the breath out of me. Oh well. At least stupid Room Three didn't win.

After the clapping has stopped, Miss Soames goes on. "The Special Incentive Award for the pair who walked the trail in the fastest time goes to Bernice Hardy and Bruce Wilmot of Room Three."

What?

"And, for their splendid effort, they will have the privilege and honour of presenting the cheque from the walk to the president of the Nationwide Save-the-Kids Fund."

Joel digs me in the side. "Fantastic prize," he sniggers.

I giggle.

"And, finally, we come to the award for the class that tried the hardest, the class that gets to go on the tour of the bread factory." Miss Soames smiles fondly in our direction.

Yep! I knew it. Ah well, at least it's better than the Special Incentive Award. I wonder if they give away free sticky buns, the ones that are covered in thick pink icing.

Later that same week, Mum tells me Wangs have changed their minds about wanting to build a new supermarket in Finslow. Instead, they are going to extend our one. They are going into clothes and household appliances. Mum is going to be the manager of the new extension. Already she is dreaming up newfangled ideas of how she can make the job benefit her new cause. And it's her weirdest cause yet. She got onto it after seeing a programme on TV about how there won't be any fish left in the sea if we don't stop pollution. So now she's into saving sardines!

"Whew. A lucky break for us, eh Matt?" whispers Dad.

I nod. Now Joel won't have to know how close we were to leaving Wansborough.

Short-Stuff, who is busy banging a pot on the floor, stops and starts clapping, as though she understands what Dad and I've been saying, as though she's glad, too.

Besides Wangs changing their minds, three other very cool things happen.

Room Five decide to share the computer with the rest of the school. Our class is having its turn all next week. I can't wait.

When we go to the bread factory, it's actually pretty cool seeing how the bread and rolls are made. Plus we're allowed lots of free samples. On the way home, I ask Joel to walk up Pine Trail with me to burn off some of the sticky buns I ate. He tells me where to go. And it's not up the trail.

But the best thing of all is the fax my mum brings home from work. It's from Duana:

> Hi guys
> You'll never guess what!
> My mother is pregnant!
> She wasn't really sick at all.
> How about that!
> She is giving up work. We're not sure where we're going to live yet. Maybe I could do some fast talking and suggest Wansborough!
> How was the walk-a-thon?
> ...etc...etc...
> Write and tell me all about it. THIS IS AN ORDER.
> ♡
> Duana

And so we do just that.

From the Author

I went on a walk-a-thon once. It was with my nine-year-old daughter and her class. I was one of the mothers who had offered to help. I have always enjoyed walking, so I thought it would be a fun day. I also thought I was in pretty good shape.

The trail was up the steepest and most winding track I have ever walked, and it was a very hot day. I started off doing well, but by lunchtime, my legs were wobbling and my back was aching.

By the end of the afternoon, I was trailing so far behind that they had to keep sending kids back to find me. Days afterwards, I still had aching feet and sore muscles. I learned how important it is to train for such an event.

The class raised a lot of money through the walk-a-thon, even if it nearly turned out to be a carry-a-mother-a-thon!

Elizabeth Pulford

From the Illustrator

I hope you enjoy *Trailblazers!* I liked the story very much and found myself thinking about my school days.

Like Duana, my family moved regularly, and the friends I made during the first ten days at a new school were very important to me. Sponsored walks, school plays, and other "extra" activities were great ways to meet people and make strong friendships, which lasted through thick and thin.

But, most of all, *Trailblazers!* reminded me that school was lots of fun (although it didn't always seem that way at the time)!

John Bennett

That's a Laugh
Queen of the Bean
Cinderfella's Big Night
The Flying Pig and the Daredevil Dog
Ants Aren't Antisocial
Charlotte's Web Page
Playing with Words

Thrills and Spills
Mountain Bike Mania
Destination Disaster
Journey to the New World
The Secret of Bunratty Castle
Happy Accidents!
The Chocolate Flier

Challenges and Choices
Call of the Selkie
Trailblazers!
The Hole in the Hill
The Good, the Bad,
    and Everything Else
On the Edge
The Willow Pattern

Our Wild World
Isn't It Cool? Discovering Antarctica
    and the Arctic
The Horse, of Course
Trapped by a Teacher
Mystery Bay
The Rain Forest
Feathery Fables

© Text by **Elizabeth Pulford**
© Illustrations by **John Bennett**
Edited by **Jennifer Waters**
Designed by **Karen Baxa Hoglund**

© 1999 Shortland Publications
All rights reserved. No part of this publication may be reproduced or transmitted in any form or by any means, electronic or mechanical, including photocopying, recording, taping, or any information storage and retrieval system, without permission in writing from the publisher.

09 08 07
10 9 8 7 6

Published in Australia and New Zealand by MIMOSA/McGraw-Hill,
8 Yarra Street, Hawthorn, Victoria 3122, Australia.
Published in the United Kingdom by Kingscourt/McGraw-Hill,
Shoppenhangers Road, Maidenhead, Berkshire SL6 2QL

Printed in China through Colorcraft Ltd., Hong Kong
ISBN 10: 0-7699-0437-8
ISBN 13: 978-0-7699-0437-5